MARI

THINGS MY CLIENTS HAVE TAUGHT ME

UPWORDS PRODUCTIONS

ISBN 978-1-105-47716-4

Published by

UPWORDS PRODUCTIONS

PO BOX 190

Newbury, OH 44065

Contents

Introduction

I wanted to write a book on hope. Hope is the substance of things not seen. It believes that life or a person can change for the better. It is not giving up even in the bleakest circumstances. Hope is using our rational minds, and our free will to try to do what is best. Kindness is best. Truth is best. Saying no to things that will hurt us or those we love is best. Getting help when we need it is best. Praying as needed is best. If I can give some hope to one hopeless person through this book, then my time has been well spent in writing it.

This book has been a long time in coming. My name is Marlene Lefton. I have a Bachelor's in social work, a Masters in Social Science Administration, and am a Licensed Independent Social Worker - Supervisor. I've been doing counseling in one form or another for over 30 years. I have done private therapy since 1992. Before that I worked in a psych hospital, alcohol rehab centers, hospital emergency/trauma center, a mental health center and the county dept. of children and family services.

This book is about my journey. It is about the things I have learned while working with people of all ages, colors, religions and personalities. My book is not so much about what a great therapist I am, it is about what I've learned from the people I've been talking to. Some lessons didn't feel so good. Sometimes I felt that I was going in circles with someone, the same issues being brought up over and over like a revolving door I was pushing, getting nowhere. The person continued to come see me, waiting for a breakthrough. Then, the difficult lesson would be taught. I 'm just a human being; I am a woman doing the best I can. I have been asking myself impossible questions. What am I doing wrong? Could someone else be doing a better job? Is this person capable of healing? I wanted to put the blame for this apparent failure on somebody or something. How hard it has been to hold onto my own words, "Not everything is somebody's fault and some things are just part of life".

Most people I only see for a short time. I want to give people tools, so they can deal with their own problems. I am not there to fix people lives or make problems cease. I want to teach skills so when difficulties do come, and they will, people will have the skills to deal with them. I do not want people to become dependent on me. I want them to have confidence in themselves and their God. The counseling process is not always totally comfortable for me or the client. I remind myself, that at the very least, I am empowering people to make their own decisions in life. I remind myself of the many people who have been able to heal in my office. I get strength to keep moving on, and hopefully that client does as well.

I enjoy it when something I have said continues to help someone. I will often hear from someone I saw, "Remember that thing you told me, it has changed my life". Those statements have encouraged me to write this book. I have asked people to send me the things I have told them that have helped them. They have sent me these "Marlene-isms" and many have been included in this book.

Marlene-ism: We are to share each other's burdens, but not each other's loads.

A burden is a real problem, a concern, where there is something to be done. Sometimes the only thing to be done is empathy, validating feelings, but it is still something we can do. A load is carrying someone's anxiety/worry, and no matter what we do or say, the other person will never view it as enough. Usually people with loads will eventually quit coming to see me. If God wants me to help someone He will give me the ability, time, and resources to help. I have learned that if I am overwhelmed, or bent down, then I am carrying something that is not mine to carry. I have to prayerfully ask what has to change. Is it my expectations or is it the situation? Sometimes, one has to wait for an answer. Practicing patience can be difficult, but I have learned, I can only teach something that I myself have learned. One cannot give something that he does not possess.

Acceptance

I see individuals, couples, and families in my counseling office. They have taught me that we all have an innate desire for someone to "understand us". What we usually mean, is that we want someone to be able to think like we do. We keep explaining things over and over hoping somehow a person will finally get what we're trying to say. We often get louder and louder as we continue to explain and explain. The concept I've learned, is that one cannot control feelings or thoughts... their own, or someone else's. We can only control our own behavior, and ask for someone else to control their own behavior. Behaviors, can be changed, or accepted as they are. Acceptance is different from understanding. Acceptance means we can give up our desire to understand a behavior. We can't always comprehend what the other person is saying but we can accept it as their reality. These concepts sound so easy and logical on paper. But I've also learned over time, that this is a hard way of living and loving. Acceptance is also knowing that we and others, will often fail. I understand why I fail and I accept why you fail. Emotions or thoughts are neither bad nor good, they just are. We cannot control them. We can only control what we do with our thoughts and emotions and how we behave.

Marlene-ism: We all have would ofs, should ofs and could ofs from our pasts.

Hopefully, we all get smarter as we age, so of course we would do things differently now. We need to not get stuck in the past and if we try to forecast the future, we do not have enough information. The only place we can do anything about is today.

A man, I shall call Bill, was ordered to counseling by his employer. He was intelligent, nice fellow, who had been self-mutilating his own body. He was obviously uncomfortable around people, and felt he in no way fit in with the rest of the world. I originally did the normal therapist thing and tried to teach him how to get along better with people. I finally got it. I had to accept him the way he was, and help him to do the same thing. When one day he told me he wanted to die, I was able to tell him what God had shown me. We are all different, but individually valuable just because that is who we are and how God has created us. Yes, I do believe that God has created each of us in his image. I told him I would do everything in my power to keep him alive. Miraculously, he said ok. I still see him, and we have come to appreciate and accept our differences. It has made for many interesting conversations.

Anger

I have learned that emotions are neither bad nor good, they just are, and it is only what we do with them that is bad or good. Well, anger is one of those emotions. Anger can be a gift, letting us know that something is wrong. If something is wrong, then something has to change. However, rage is out of control anger, and it is never good. I started seeing a man over ten years ago. He was on parole for many fights including assaulting several police officers at one time. Parole is something one does after prison. He was seeing me as a condition of parole, and it was clear he did not want to be there. He made fun of my profession, and "accidentally" broke some objects in my office. He was someone I wish I didn't have to see as well. I finally had had enough, and told him he was making it hard for me to like him. I said that in my office my client's and I mutually respected each other and that I was not used to being treated so poorly. He was shocked. He had never heard a person talk of mutual respect or that he could be in some way victimizing me. He had been abused in some way from everyone who had ever counseled or parented him from early childhood on. My words shocked him. I was expressing my desire to give him dignity. Something changed that day. We did learn to mutually respect each other. I still see him as needed, and I enjoy him when he comes to see me. We make each other smile.

Similarly, I had a female lady, who I will call Susie, who also was ordered by the court into counseling after spending many months at the county jail. This was not her first jail experience. She was described as angry and hostile by all systems working with her. I was told by various persons that they had to go through the motions of ordering counseling, but did not really expect me to be able to help her. Susie was in fact an angry woman with a cuss word in every sentence. But, she was funny, and made me laugh frequently. The more I laughed, the more relaxed she became. Soon she was no longer cussing, but was crying between jokes. This lady started sharing her deepest wounds. Lo and behold, she was also abused in various ways her whole life. I was the only one who ever laughed with her, and not at her. She saw me on and off for several years. Susie finally married her boyfriend, whom had asked her many times before. She had always said no in the past, because she couldn't believe anyone could love her. She obtained employment, got her children back from county custody, and never got in trouble with the law again. She calls me every now and then or will send a card, just to let me know she is doing well. Both of the above clients also came to believe that

God above also loves them. A concept they could never grasp before.

And speaking about swearing.... I have never told a person not to swear, but I do not swear. It is interesting to me how every person I have seen has either stopped swearing altogether, or has cut back on their cussing greatly while in my office. This has been true even for teenagers. The obvious lesson here is, actions speak louder than words. Another lesson here is that people need to be accepted, appreciated, and respected as they are, not as you want them to be. I once overheard an angry psychotic gentleman talking with a co-worker. It was clear, that this new co-worker was having a difficult time calming this enraged fellow. I walked into her office and overheard her trying to talk the man out of his delusion. He was telling her he had just returned from the planet "Nexum" and was too tired to be answering her questions. I knew he needed to be seen by the psychiatrist to receive medications to help relieve his hallucinations. Having him see the Doctor was the only way we were going to help him. I validated that he must be tired from his long trip and he could relax in the waiting room until the doctor was ready to see him. I knew all was well when he said to me, "I think I know you. Have you ever been to the planet Nexum?" I answered honestly, "No, I don't think I have". He then got up and waited in the waiting room for the psychiatrist.

Fear

I learned much about anxiety from the "milk therapy" lady. I was working on the crises line at a mental health facility. An elderly woman called frantically repeating, "I don't know what to do". She told me she had called every agency in town and they didn't know what to do either. She could not verbalize what was making her so anxious. I asked her questions about her safety. She was able to tell me that she lived with her son and he was coming home from work shortly. I knew she was safe. I told her I knew what to do. She instantly became relieved and said thank God someone knows what to do. I had calmed her fears and now had to come up with the 'what to do' part. I asked her if she had milk in the house. When she said yes, I was able to reassure her she would definitely be ok. The plan was for her to pour herself a glass of milk, rest on the couch, and call me back in fifteen minutes. She said she would do exactly as I said. It worked. She called me back 15 minutes later and had calmed down. She was now able to express the real cause of her anxiety. She was recently released from the hospital after a fall and had to go live with her son. She felt confused, being away from everything familiar to her, and physically helpless. She needed someone to reassure her she would be ok and still had the ability to do some things for herself. I had responded to the fear in her voice in a calm, rational way, and did not turn her away just because she could not tell me what was wrong.

People have asked me if I have ever been afraid. The answer to that question is a resounding, yes. However, I have never made a decision based on my fears. Once I was in the hospital emergency room. At that time I had the power to "pink slip", which is a pink piece of paper one would fill out. This form allowed the police or ambulance to be able to take someone to the psychiatric hospital for an evaluation of up to three days, even against their will. I had been called to the emergency room to do a mental health evaluation on this client. This man had tried to overdose and was in a hospital bed with intravenous fluid in his arm. I had heard he was agitated and had asked hospital security and the police to stay in the room with me while I did his assessment. He was still suicidal and delusional and so I pinked slipped him. He stood up and pulled his I.V. out of his arm. He then turned to me with an angry glare and a finger pointed at me and said, "YOU. If you hospitalize me I will track you down and eventually will kill you." I yelled back, with knees shaking, "Sit down", and he did. There were three things that gave me courage at that moment; 1) my Higher Power, 2) the handful of armed security guards and police in that room, 3) when he stood up his hospital gown fell off. He was standing there naked and jumping up and down. Inside I was not only shaking with fear but also laughter at the sight. I was still laughing as I left the room. I learned we are all the same underneath our clothes, (slightly different for men and women) and laughter really is the best medicine.

Another time I had a father come to see me for a court custody evaluation on his two children. Over the years I had done many custody evaluations. One child was a boy about nine years of age, and his sister was about seven years of age. It has always been my policy to see the children first by themselves without parents to not bias the children. The children were sweet and adorable. It was only at the end of our session, when they began to trust me that they told me how afraid they were of their mother and her family. They cried hard as they told me of the abuse they had suffered. They adored their father and were very happy since their mom had left them. Both begged me not to let mom or her family come back in their lives. I then asked to speak with dad. It was at that point that dad told me the mom and her family's story. After dad had married his wife, he discovered that her family were gangsters, the kind that actually had their enemies killed. He did not tell me this before as he was rightfully concerned that I would not take his case if I knew of his wife's family. At first I thought he was kidding. But after speaking with his lawyer and the man's pastor I discovered this was indeed the truth. All involved were fearful that someone would shoot them to keep them from testifying. What should I do? Should I join the group and agree to testify? I knew that if I did not agree to go to court, that there was a good chance these children would be forced to visit with their mom. I could not shake the picture of the children tearfully pleading with me to rescue them. After much prayer and soul searching, I did go to the courtroom with fear racing through my body. There were several armed court security guards there to protect the judge, the lawyer, the pastor, the father and me. You will be glad to know, that there were no violin cases anywhere. No one even showed up from the mother's side of the family. We all testified before the judge. The verdict was that dad got sole custody and all visitations with mom and her family was outlawed.

Not knowing what is going to happen in life can be a bit scary. Decisions based on fear or anxieties are not usually good decisions. Most things that make us afraid don't ever happen. Consequently, anxiety that something bad might happen is not a good reason to not try something. If something bad happens, and it probably won't, with God's help we will find a way to deal with the situation. Concerns are another matter. Concerns are based on facts. A concern means we have enough information to do something differently and then we can let it go. Anxieties or fears of the future can stay with us no matter what we decide to do in the present.

People of all ages can be afraid. Children's fears are as real to them as adult's fears are to adults. Children have taught me how to enter their world with them. One 6 year old child I saw was refusing to go to school. The child was unable to put her fears into word, but I could tell they were real to her none the less. Instead of trying to talk her out of her worries, which is an adult strategy, I decided to speak her language. I remembered a song I learned a long time ago called "The Nothing Song". The chorus to this song is;

"Nothing, nothing, nothing, nothing...nothing, nothing all day long...absolutely nothing, nothing...How'd you like my nothing song?"

I taught this girl this silly song. We both laughed as we sang. I then prefaced our song with the statement, "guess what is going to happen to you when you go to school tomorrow?   And then answered in a loud voice, NOTHING! And then we would sing our song again and again. I had become a part of her world. I was validating that I understood that she was afraid of something she did not have words for. I was able to put the answer to her unspoken fears into a silly song, and was willing to sing the silly answer with her. Next I brought her mom into the room, and helped her become a part of this world also.

We did this routine 2 weeks in a row in my office, while mom did this routine with her daughter every morning at home. Going to school each morning now became a time for giggles instead of crying…and in only two weeks. I learned from this child that children need children solutions, not adult solutions.

Another 6 year old child also taught me a valuable lesson, this one was a boy. He also had fears he could not put into words. His mom was pregnant and was to soon have a Cesarean delivery. His parents had explained him, that a cesarean delivery meant the doctor would be cutting open his mother's stomach to remove the baby. This boy had insisted on sleeping next to his mother every night. Parents brought the boy to me to help determine and stop this night time behavior, before the new baby was born. I knew I had to enter his world if I was going to help him. When I entered his world it became clear that he was not trying to manipulate his parents, but was afraid to leave his mother's side. During our time together, the boy also shared with me his fascination with spiders. And that his pet spider had recently died. He had read many books on spiders and had seen many nature specials on the subject. We kept talking and eventually the mystery unfolded. In this young child's mind, the obstetrician was going to slice his mother's belly open and maybe spiders would come out instead of a human child. I then explained how God ordained only spiders to come out of spiders, and human babies to come out of humans. This was the facts of life explained in a concrete six year old mentality. This was the comfort he was looking for. He became able to sleep in his own room without fear. This child reminded me to keep asking questions and to really listen to answers.

Children

In my office, I see all people six years old and up. You are probably wondering, why would a six year old child need to see a counselor? Some are children whose parents have gotten divorced or have left in some other fashion. Yes, unless there was actual abuse, children, no matter how old they are, always hope that their parents would stay together. You see, children and teens are, by nature, consumed with their own world and worries. Parents need to give to their children (and I am not speaking here about physical presents) and must only expect to receive back from them when the children become adults. Other children I have seen have been physically or sexually abused. Some have some form of mental illness, neurological disorder or a learning disability. Some parents bring their child, not knowing what is wrong, but knowing their behavior is very odd or difficult. Sometimes we will play games; board games, card games, made up games. Sometimes we will just talk. Something they don't teach one in graduate school is how to have fun. With children that is the whole key in helping them. There must be fun, fun, fun. They have to feel that they are special, you are extremely interested in what they have to say, and they must enjoy themselves. I laugh at their jokes, make up a few of my own, and will play any game that they choose. Kids are often starved for this kind of adult attention in our busy world. Getting knowledge for an assessment and imparting words of wisdom must be done within the above framework. I try to teach parents to do some of the same. Parents will tell me their children told them that coming to my office were the best times they have ever had. It helps the adults to know that their children are not feeling damaged by coming to see me.

Another childhood/teen trauma is getting bullied in school. A bully is someone who repeatedly forces a child/teen to do things they do don't want to do, or continues to taunt others to make them look bad. Another requirement of bullying is that the child/teen has no way of stopping it. This behavior can also occur between siblings. Most adults, in our great wisdom, tell kids to just walk away or ignore them. When one is trapped in school for forty hours a week, for eighteen years, with the same people over and over again, that advice is almost impossible to follow. These are also the same peers one is supposed to spend time with all weekends and at school activities. I have learned that these children need an adult to be their advocate. Schools and parents need to have a no bullying policy, be alert to any signs it is occurring, and have consistent consequences to stop it. Schools cannot rely on the victims to report such behavior. Tattle telling can cause someone to be victimized all over again. I have learned to intervene over the years as needed. I will often call on the phone, write a letter, or call a school meeting to address this issue. Sometimes, adults putting their heads and eyes together can devise plans to stop this behavior.

Another problem for children can be blended families. Most families today fall somewhere within this category. Remember, just because your partner is the love of your life, your child may not feel the same way about him or her. The adults in the home need to make the rules and consequences together. The rules can be presented to the children together. Then the rules become the authority figure. This is important as it is often difficult for children to see the non-biological parent as an authority figure. Parents often change their partners several times. Children/teens have a hard time switching parental figures even one time.

Teamwork

Another lesson I have learned is to be a team player. I have tried to help parents work as team with their children and I try to take my own advice. If adults are not on the same page children will divide and conquer. This same principle is true in the adult world. Abraham Lincoln once said, "A nation divided against itself cannot stand". My clients are often involved with court systems, county children and family services, probation officers, other mental health professionals, other drug and alcohol systems, or various insurance companies. I try to collaborate, with the client's permission, with the various systems involved, to make sure we are all on the same page. I do not always agree with others involved, but will discuss things in a respectful way. I remember to change the things I can and accept the things I can't change. I can only teach lessons I have learned myself.

Once I called an insurance company when I had concerns about a suicidal client. I felt he needed an in-patient facility, a higher level of care than I could provide. They had an emergency contact person and phone number that I did not have. This person was called and she went over to the client's home. She found the man unconscious and called 911. The man was taken by ambulance to the hospital emergency room and then placed in an in-patient facility. Today, this man is doing well. He is grateful that the insurance company and I, with the grace of God, saved his life.

Grief

Grieving the loss of someone, especially through death, is never done in the same way. I worked for a time in the emergency room/trauma center in a major hospital. Part of my job was locating family members, requesting they come to the hospital, and helping them once they were there. Most people are in shock when you first tell them their loved one has been in a terrible accident.

A man had been life-flighted, flown by helicopter, to our hospital. His small plane had crashed and I explained to her that over half his body had been burned. His wife wanted to know if he would be home for supper that evening. I told her that he would be in the hospital for a while and it would be best if she could find someone to bring her to him.

A man on a motorcycle, who was not wearing a helmet, was brought in DOA, dead on arrival. He son could not be comforted. He was wailing, beating his head against the wall. Suddenly, he smiled. He had decided how he could honor his father and this gave him peace. He was going to use his dad's motorcycle as a monument at the gravesite.

Knowing his dad and bike would be together forever brought him comfort.

Some nationalities grieved loudly, bringing every relative to the hospital to say good bye. Others grieved quietly, wanting to say good bye privately. Most looked for some spiritual consolation while seeing a loved one passing from death to life. Fortunately for these families, we could give them freedom of religion, and not insist on freedom from religion. Death is not a time to argue whether someone was created or evolved from some other life form. I have learned to not argue this in life either. I am tolerant of all positions. I have my own opinion that we were created, and you can have your opinion. Working in the hospital and seeing how complicated the human body has only confirmed this belief for me. Another lesson learned; one never knew who would live or die. There were so many surprises for all of the staff, someone dying who one thought would surely live, and some living who one thought would surely die. There is always hope.

Life

In the Trauma Center, one never knew who would live or die. There were so many surprises for all of the staff, someone dying who one thought would surely live, and some living who one thought would surely die. There is always hope.

And speaking of hope, I never give up on anyone. I saw an alcoholic lady who had three failed suicide attempts. One of those attempts was while I was seeing her. When she called me asking if she could return for counseling, she was surprised when I said yes. Eventually she did quit drinking, got married, moved out of state, and had three beautiful children. She kept in touch for years through phone calls, letters and e-mails. She was one grateful lady. Her words were, "I am praising God and thanking you daily for my beautiful life and family. I am trying to give to others all the knowledge and peace I have been given".

I have learned that every life is a precious gift. A man called on the crisis hot-line at 4:50pm. We were supposed to close at 5:00PM. He had a loaded gun to his head and wanted me to give him one good reason why he should not pull the trigger. I kept him on the phone for one and a half hours while my co-workers called the police who traced the call. I prayed while thinking that at any minute I would hear the gun go off. The police SWAT team arrived on the scene. They told him to put the gun down. Again, any minute I expected to hear a gun go off. He was screaming at me how I had betrayed him. Good, I thought. He is talking and not shooting. In a loud but firm voice I told him to put the gun down and that I wanted to have the chance to meet this nice, funny man I had been talking with for an hour and a half. There was a moment of silence that seemed to last an eternity in my mind. He said ok and gave the gun to the policeman. He made an appointment to see me for counseling. I was fearful when he first came in that he might shoot me. I saw him for 2 years. He thanked me for helping him. He had a spiritual awakening, and reconnected with family members. Years later I got a call from another crisis counselor. She said the same man told her to call me, as he was suicidal, and I would know what to say to talk him out of it. You'll be glad to know he again did not kill himself.

Marriage

Marriage is an emotional, financial, spiritual, and legal commitment we make to a partner. It is supposed to last a lifetime, and when it doesn't, there is a ripping apart for children, finances, extended family, and friends. Many people get hurt. I am always in favor of trying to make a marriage work, unless there is some sort of abuse occurring. A concurring belief is that people need to live in a safe place where fear does not abound. As long as both partners, and sometimes it is only one partner, continue to see me, I will continue to work towards that goal. I have seen couples reconcile who were actually working on divorces, or had already been divorced or separated. I have had many couples tell me, "We have seen other counselors, but hear you are a different kind of therapist, and you are our last resort". The lesson here to me is if I actually believe in the sanctity of marriage people will sense it and respond differently. Have all couples I have seen stayed together? The answer is no. Have I seen most couples stay together? The answer is a resounding yes.

I have learned many lessons from these married clients which also can apply to all relationships. I will restate what I said earlier because it is so important. We want someone to "understand" us. What we really mean is we want others to be able to think like us. People keep explaining things over and over in the hope that someone will finally get it and finally agree. It is much like speaking to someone in a foreign language. Getting louder, or repetition, does still not translate a foreign language into English. We need each other to "accept" the differences, or agree to disagree. A person cannot control their own or another's thoughts or feelings. One can only control behavior, which is what we or they do with thoughts or feelings. Negotiating and compromising, the same skills used in a business, is what is needed. When there is a company strike, or a divorce, everyone loses.

Marlene-ism: Relationships need maintenance.

If a car does not get oil changes, the engine will eventually stop running. No one will see the engine dying, but die it will. A garden weeded and a home repaired. If people don't make the time to talk or have fun, the relationship will fall apart. We cannot put people on hold. Things can be repaired once broken, but it will take more time and effort. Do the maintenance.

Marlene-ism: Behaviors change, before feelings do.

The saying, "Fake it till you make it", actually works in real life. Often people want someone to do something only if they want to. In fact, people need to do something even if they don't want to. Emotions and thoughts are neither bad nor good, they just are. Behavior is the thing to work on, individually and as a couple. I often make family members complement each other in my office. Many times they are reluctant to comply as they are feeling angry and defensive. When I can persuade them to do it anyways, they always become softer towards each other. The exchanging of kind words, a behavior, causes their thoughts and feelings of anger and defensiveness to change.

I began to understand that behaviors repeated often enough, begin to feel normal and becomes habits. A habit is something we repeat without thinking about it. For example, try folding your arms a different way, tough huh? People daily put their pants on and off the same way and hygiene routines stay the same. We have also "learned in habits" in ways of dealing with emotions. It takes energy and concentration to break and change an old habit. Children are great motivators for changing. Whatever we don't deal with, our children do. The bad habits that we don't break will feel normal to our children and they will most likely repeat them. Parents have more power to change the atmosphere in the home than the children do. Children learn more by what they see than what they hear. Children have a keen sixth sense for hypocrisy. Whatever we are not willing to deal with; our children will have to deal with, for example, pain.

Happiness

It's important to have fun. One assignment I like to give to any relationship that is in trouble, is to do something together that is fun. We were not created to be serious continuously. There is God given pleasure chemicals that are released when we laugh, "A cheery heart is good medicine for the soul". There is a positive bond that is created when we enjoy each other's company. There are good memories that are created and become etched in the brain. A sight, sound, smell, can evoke these positive memories to come to the surface causing us to smile all over again. In our busy world, if we don't put fun time on the calendar, we usually don't make time for it. Spontaneity is good, but it does not happen often enough. Many people lose the ability to make merry naturally, and so, addictions have become rampant. I personally, love to laugh. I model this ability when appropriate, and hope that people can take this gift home with them and use it. I smile as I write this and hope dear reader you are also smiling. How can I laugh with all of the problems I listen to daily? I do not laugh at the problems, but in between them. It is important to learn to put time aside, no matter how difficult life becomes, to just smell the roses. It is the only way we can cope when we return our attention to problem solving. Some people call this compartmentalizing, others call it choosing to forget for a short while, some call it legging go and letting God, and others might call it distraction. When I lose my ability to smile I will know that it is time to quit my job. I can also keep smiling because I have hope. When people come to see me and they feel hopeless, I tell them they can borrow my hope for a while. I have seen so many people and situations change for the better, that I am never hopeless. If I become hopeless, then that is another sign I have to quit my job.

Marlene-ism: A key to happiness is to set high goals for ourselves, but low expectations for others.

Pain

Let's talk about pain. First principle is that God never wastes pain.

Marlene-ism: You don't get well going around pain. You have to go straight through it to heal.

All of us need to learn to sit in some pain some of the time. Not all pain is bad. There is good pain and there is bad pain. Getting stabbed in the chest is bad if it happens to someone during a bank robbery, but in can be a good thing if it is open heart surgery. Both acts may feel the same at the time, but one produces something bad, the other can produce something good.

I have always thought that suicide is a person's desire to remove their pain and that there are always other options to remove the pain. Hopefully the client will agree to work out other options with me before they will try killing themselves. One brave client did just that. She gave me a copy of her journal chronicling this process after she decided to live. I will let you read some of it as well.

"I believe it was during this time that I just wanted to die. I wrote a suicide letter to my son with instructions as to

where he could find my legal documents and how much I loved him. Then I went to bed to think about how to do this. Thank goodness I had the time to think about how I was going to plan my death, because I ended up reasoning myself out of going through with it, and once again I called my mental health therapist, Marlene. I am better now. I'm feeling better now. What an emotional roller coaster ride it was. I just had to let some things go and I'm still working on the rest of the issues. I'm a continual work in progress".

This client taught me that my slogan to suicidal clients, "you can always do that, but let's try some other things first", is a good one. When they have no hope left, I tell them that I have enough hope for the both of us. My clients have taught me that there is always hope, I have been allowed to see that hope lived out in many lives. It encourages me and them.

There is a purpose in pain. It is God's way of letting us know something is wrong. What's wrong could be the situation itself, or it could be my expectations. I must decide what needs to change. Needing change and taking the right course of action can be painful in the short run, but it feels so good when we are through it. If we live long enough, something we don't like will happen. It can be a health problem, or a financial problem, or a family problem or a "you fill in the blank" problem. It is not the problems that break us; it is the inability to deal with them. Don't be afraid of pain, use it well.

Teens

Pre-teens are emotionally challenged. Their hormones and their moods are up and down. Their message to each other and their families is "go away/come back". Since they are all locked up together in a school, with hundreds or thousands of other emotionally challenged pre-teens and teens 5 days a week, their days can be very stressful. This can also make it stressful on the entire families of pre-teens. I can see this same behavior in my office. So, I have learned to not fight them, but join them. If they will not talk to me, I bring the parent in, and we ignore them. I ask the parent questions about their child. Invariable, the child who has refused to talk, will suddenly yell, "That is not what happened, my parent is wrong". I will then ask the pre-teen to tell me how they see the situation, and they actually want to join the conversation. One girl was court ordered to see me. She would have gone to detention home if she had left my office. She also refused to speak to me. I turned my back on her and started doing paper work. She screamed, "Are you going to do that the entire hour?" I turned to her and said," The choice is yours. #1, we can talk. #2, we can play a game. #3, I can continue to do paper work." She chose #2 and in the process we also did #1.

Families can do themselves a favor and not take any of this unpredictable behavior personally. The parent figure has to stay calm and stay connected; while the pre-teen is bouncing back and forth, trying to figure themselves and life out. I have had several of these bouncing pre-teens refer their friends to me, a high compliment, and a sign I was practicing what I preach.

The biggest lesson for teens to learn is that, with freedom comes responsibility. And since teens must learn this lesson, there must be adults who are willing to teach it. Parents must be consistent and willing to give consequences. Discipline and authority are not popular words in our culture today. If we can think of discipline as accountability and authority as leadership, then these words can have positive connotations. Every person, including myself, needs an accountability partner to speak truth to us, and help keep us on the right path. Every organization needs good, strong, moral leaders with a clear vision that followers can believe in. These characteristics do not develop overnight. They are taught and caught over an extended period of time. Parental discipline is not about punishing, it is about teaching.

I tell teens that they will have to listen to people and do as they are told their whole life. That is, if they want to keep a job and stay out of jail. Every teen wants to be rich and buy lots of things, but most don't have a clue how to get there. I point out that our bosses have the right to fire us, our government has the right to prosecute us, our teachers have the right to fail us, and parents have the right to take things away. I explain to the parents and the teens that the law only mandates food, clothing, and shelter; NOT phones, iPods, games, TV, face book, name brand products, sports, and the like. It is usually a novel concept to teens *and their parents* that the parents can refuse to buy these products or take them away. The initial shock turns into awe as I explain that these products are privileges which should be earned. We do not allow children to develop into successful adults if we spoil them and make them feel like the world owes them luxuries or unwilling to earn rewards. I actually enjoy working with teens. They keep me real and authentic. They pick up on any inconsistencies and will call you out on any hypocrisy. Unlike some adults, they do not expect all people to lie, and will "diss" you if you do.

All people need clear expectations, and a knowledge of what will happen if these expectations are not met. With children and teens, the 1, 2, 3, method works well. The first time we ask them to follow the rules, the second time we calmly remind them if the rule is not followed the consequence will ensue, and the third time the consequence is enforced. This method works best if A) the rule has been fully explained earlier when all were calm, B) the consequence has also been fully explained when all were calm and C) the consequence fits the crime and can be easily enforced. Short and sweet is important. No long lectures which get tuned out, and short take-a-ways, so time can easily be added to the penance if needed.

When teens tell me how they are as smart as adults and don't need any advice. I ask them if they are smarter now than they were one year ago, or two years ago. This especially works well if they have a younger sibling or cousin. They can always say they are definitely smarter than these others. And so I logically remind them that they will know more next year and the year after. Even the teens can now relate to the fact that since their parents have lived longer than they have, parents might know a few more things than they do. I enjoy working with teens. They keep me honest, and keep me real. They have many qualities that I want to hold on to as I age.

Addictions

I have seen people who have received several DUIs (driving under the influence) and gone to jail for them, people who have lost their homes, or jobs, or families, etc. but still feel like they are not like those other people who go to meetings. Somehow people to want to believe that they are not as bad as the other guy. This detrimental aspect is what we in the field call denial. We can see poor behavior in others but are able to ignore, minimize, rationalize, blame others, and otherwise explain away our own poor behavior. It is especially hard to show someone how they are one or two steps away from losing all, if they have not already done so. I worked with a gentleman who lost his license and his car, spent time in jail, and had spent thousands of dollars in court related expenses, including coming to see me. He stated that he couldn't relate to anyone at the AA meetings, as they were a bunch of losers. I tried to point out how he appeared to be heading down the same path. He emphatically told me, NO WAY. He believed he had everything under control. The next week he come in to see me he had lost his job after flunking a random drug/alcohol test. People actually believe drinking a six pack or two or three is common, and "everybody does it". They are shocked when I mention that most of the people I know do not do this. No one starts out to be addict. It is just a series of making one poor choice after another. It is wonderful to see a light bulb go off with some of my clients when they begin to realize that mental health is just making one right choice after the next.

The Marlene way of explaining addiction; 1) A truly social drinker plans out their social drinking. A person will have one or two drinks. He/she will have a designated driver if needed. There will be no dangerous situations and no mess to clean up. If a social drinker believes they can never drink again it is no big deal. 2) A binge drinker, or alcohol abuser sometimes will do as above, but other times will not. They will sometimes drink way too much or won't have a designated driver. The will at times be in a dangerous situation or will have a big mess to clean up. The gentleman I mentioned previously fell into this category. This group is the hardest people to convince that they have a serious problem. They usually tell me they can quit any time that they want. I then ask them why they don't quit when it seems to be dangerous not to. I ask is it worth the risk? The answers vary and so does the prognosis. 3) The person is alcohol dependent. Some people believe that this is the only group that is truly an alcoholic. They need alcohol to even just feel normal.

A Marlene-ism: An addict is someone that does something over and over again, even though the behaviors cause problems and interfere with functioning.

Logically a person would quit a behavior if it caused severe problems. The fact that a person cannot quit a behavior leads me to believe that they are an addict. The addiction as above can be to alcohol or drugs. But by Marlene's definition other things can also be equally devastating. Other addictions can include gambling, raging, shopping, pornography, shopping, sex, work, or even falling in love. It is the need to do it over and over and the hurtful consequences that make it an addiction. Addictions do not just affect the addict, but also anyone that cares about or has trust in the addict. Addictions begin as a way to try and escape pain, or to numb out, or to fit in. After a while the addiction takes on a life of its own, and one does it because they are addicted, even though the addict will often attempt to blame others for their behavior. Someone can disappoint or anger or frustrate a person, but no forces a person to do a certain behavior. We all get disappointed, etc., but not everyone acts out.

Fighting

Rules of fighting fair. Fair fighting is an important skill. It is the means of solving conflicts. Raging and the silent treatment are the flip sides of the same coin. Both shut down communication. There are some things we can do that will increase the odds of creating a win/win situation in a conflict. Compromise is meeting someone in the middle, or taking turns giving in to a situation. Here are some of the rules I have learned: 1) no raising voices, this will make some people shut down 2) no name calling 3) no swearing 4) no put downs 5) stay in the present i.e. no bring up the past 6) no monologues, dialogues instead 7) one topic at a time, no linking, 8) keep other people out of the conversation 9) take time outs as needed 10) reach a compromise.

What is a time out? Good timing is necessary for fair fighting. If either person is unable to keep the above rules, he/she can call a time out. It is a time to walk away and calm down. One can count to ten, pray, meditate, exercise, listen to music etc.; and to return when able to keep the mouth shut or fair fight. It is hoped the person who took the time out will reschedule the fair fighting at a later date. Remember, if conflict doesn't get solved, they don't just go away on their own. Why is it important to stay in the present? We cannot change the past, and so it becomes a circular argument. Linking is jumping from subject to subject; you did that, oh yeh, well you do this and that; again, a circular argument. Solve one problem, and at a later date the other person can bring up their complaint. When people complain that these rules are too hard, we go back to options and possible outcomes. Usually they determine that their way of dealing with conflict got them to my office and the possibility of divorce. They decide to try the new deal. I remind them that they probably do these things automatically at work, or with friends or neighbors. Usually they agree, and now realize they do have the skills they need to do this at home.

One technique I use to teach people to fight fair is the ball technique. That is when the person who is holding their ball in his/her hand is the only one allowed to talk. The other person must listen and not speak. After a couple of sentences, the ball must be passed. Now the person listening must repeat back what the first person said, before he/she can answer. The process continues until the problem is solved. Couples counseling is not about me stating who is wrong or right, but it is for me to teach communication skills. Men and women are relieved when they discover they are not going to get beat up in my office. If someone gets too heated, I get the ball and I am the only one who can speak. This method forces a couple of positive outcomes. People learn they cannot just interrupt each other which is the way most people have discussions. People also are forced to listen and not just prepare their own rebuttal, as they have to repeat back what the other has said before they are permitted to answer. If the couple breaks the other fair fighting rules, I take the ball, remind them of the rule, and then give it back. We keep the ball rolling until a compromise is reached. Often they will say, "This is a stupid argument; let's talk about something that is really important". I calmly state that the fact that they can't solve a "stupid argument" is something really important. The issue then usually gets quickly resolved, and each success breeds another success.

Behaviors

If someone presents me with some drastic action they are ready to perform, I have learned to help them not to feel boxed into making a black or white decision. For example, if they have a suicidal thought, or a divorce inclination, I mention, "you can always do that, let's try something else first". As we work on new coping methods, their desire for drastic reaction leaves, and they learn how to compromise, (shades of grey). Trying to talk someone out of their feelings or thoughts is useless. This blowing of hot air just makes a person's thoughts or feelings more entrenched. If I tell you NOT to think of a pink elephant, of course that is the first thing you will think about. If I can help you to put the thought aside for a time, then we can try to instill new behaviors. Often new thoughts and feelings follow new behaviors. If I wait till I feel like quitting an addiction, I often will never quit. If I wait till I feel like being nice to you, I often will never be nice. Kindness is contagious, and so is cruelty. This concept is the basis of all anti-bullying programs. When we are not acting out our emotions, it forces us to put them into words and hopefully fight fair. We can see how foolish children look when they don't fight fair in our homes or on the playground: "That's mine, is not, is too" or "I hate you, well I hate you, well I hate you more", or worse yet, "go away, NOBODY likes you". Yet as adults we can fight the same way. Only, we use bigger words, bigger sentences, and fight over bigger subjects. We need to re-parent ourselves as we parent our children. Even if we do not have children we still can have the opportunity re-parent ourselves as adults. When we force ourselves to fight fair, or be nice, or walk away, or put our feelings into words, we are re-parenting ourselves into healthy adults.

Communication

Do I give advice? I call it exploring options. We discuss all possible options and the possible outcomes of each choice; and then the person has to choose their own option. After all, they are the ones that have to live with their choices, not me. Sometimes I am asked questions I cannot answer. A question I hear repeatedly is, "How can I make him or her stop lying"? I always reply, "I don't know". Instead of giving a command, such as "you can't", I again go through options and possible outcomes. Each person must come to their own conclusions.

Opinions are only helpful if a person wants to hear one. It is important to ask someone first if he/she wants to hear our opinion before we pontificate. If a person says no, then we have to respect their wishes. Hopefully, they will do the same for us. This is a hard lesson to learn. I have learned from my clients that communication is about speaking the other person's language. Speaking is only a one way lecture unless we find a way to be heard. Repeating ourselves, long lectures, raising voices, and put downs, may make us feel more powerful; but, how powerful are we if the other person has tuned us out?

I remember a teenage girl whose mother brought her to see me bi-weekly. She would just sit in my office as if she was staring off into space and I would talk, doing mostly a monologue. I would talk about problem-solving, things from her past and things for her future to dream about. The mother asked if she should continue to bring her daughter. I told mom to continue to bring this young teenage girl to my office as long as she would be willing to come. I had seen something in her eyes that made me hope and partially believe that maybe this girl was actually listening to me. She quit coming to see me after several months, when I had decided I had "taught her", actually through my own monologue, as much as I could. I chalked this whole experience up to knowing that I could not help everyone, and I was doing the best I could. Several years later, this young lady called me. She told me how much she had learned from our time together. She thanked me, said she was doing well, and asked if she could make a referral one of her friends to me. The lesson for me was to look into a person eyes and soul, and not just listen to their words.

Generations

I saw a young man and his wife. Their marriage was on the rocks. They were both willing to do whatever it took to save their marriage, Ten years later they are still happily married and have five children. Because their marriage improved his mother soon began seeing me marriage and adult children of alcoholics' issues. She became emotionally healthy, her marriage improved, and her other two sons started seeing me for problems which had been passed down from generation to generation. This family was determined to break this cycle. They had learned the lesson that whatever we don't deal with, our children do. There are now eight grandchildren that will be raised in healthy homes and not have to deal with generational issues.

Then, one by one this brave woman's four siblings began seeing me. We even had a couple of family sessions. Each sibling worked hard at kicking out their own "demons" from their past. Again their children and grandchildren will be freed from generational bondage. I also had the privilege of seeing their friends and their friend's families. I gave all of them tools to solve problems in a healthy way. It is not the problems that cause the greatest misery, but the inability to solve them. God give each of us many gifts to use in this life.

These clients have taught me that our actions have ripple effects. We do not live in a vacuum, but in community one with another. What we do or say has the power to hurt many or help many. We pass down to many generations the lessons we get right and the lessons we get wrong. The good news is that it is never too late to change what messages we want to send to others. Yes, people are watching.

Forgiveness

Marlene-ism: Forgiveness means letting go of the desire to punish back. It is not reconciliation, which means restoring the original relationship.

Forgiveness is an issue that often gets brought up. Forgiveness is the act of just one person; reconciliation takes the actions of two. In order for us to let go of our anger, we must first know what we are angry about. People want to go around this pain and too quickly just move on to the letting go part. It doesn't work. We need to understand the hurt and pain the other person caused us so we can actually heal from it. I often suggest they write a letter that they will never send. The letter is to be written to the offender. It is to state the specific offenses, how the person felt then when it happened, and how they feel now thinking about it. It is to be a stream of consciousness. Grammar, chronological order, or specifics do not matter. There are a few rules: 1) don't reread, 2) no apologies for the client's inappropriate behavior, 3) no excuses for the perpetrator's problems. They are to bring the letter back to me. The client then decides which one of us will read it out loud. This helps the person to see the connection between the events of the past and the way the client feels, thinks, or behaves today. Once this pain is experienced by the conscious brain, it is now capable of letting it go. The pain no longer has the power it once had. The perpetrator's power can now also be let go. A person no longer has to spend so much emotional energy wishing to punish. Knowing that "Vengeance is Mine Sayeth the Lord", is a freeing concept.

Reconciliation is another story. One does not want to continue to be hurt. We still need boundaries. A boundary is a safe distance we must keep from an unsafe person. An unsafe person is someone who will keep doing hurtful behavior repeatedly. This person must also recognize and admit the specifics of what he/she did, how it made you feel then, and how it affects you now. A generic apology of "I'm sorry" does not cut it. Once the true apology is made, it is still up to the offended whether or not they feel safe to reconcile. After all, they are not a victim any longer, nor do they want to act like one.

Not only is forgiveness of others good for our mental health, forgiveness of self is also an important concept. To err is human. The only one who is perfect is God. We forget that concept. God often refers to us as His sheep. Sheep are dumb animals. They will follow each other to their death. They will continually get lost, thus needing a shepherd to look for them and bring them back to the fold. I am told that if they are not sheared they can fall over from the weight of their own fleece.

Marlene-ism: We are all dumb sheep.

I do not pretend to be better than anyone I counsel. I let people know that all the things I teach are things I have had to learn myself. I do not pretend to never make mistakes or to be perfect. I tell them I have learned skills and have tools that I would like to impart to them. I can teach them the skills, but I can't give them the desire to want to learn. The desire to change has to come from within them. We are all capable of changing if we want to. It is never too late and we are never too old. So how does this all apply to guilt? If we accept the notion that we will all err, and that we are not as smart or clever as we think we are, then we can also accept the notion that we will all goof. And if we expect ourselves and each other to goof, then we can forgive the goofer. Abusing and goofing are two separate concepts. An abuser is calculated and doesn't care that he/she inflicts pain. Sheep do stupid things that cause harm to themselves and others, but are not even aware of what they are doing is wrong.

Epilogue

There is not enough space in one book to write all of the things my clients have taught me. Many times my clients have taught others by saying," a friend or family member was having a problem and I told them what you told me and it really helped". We have all learned that we don't have to be perfect to help others. In fact, good things can come out of our own pain. Most of the tools I teach others have come out of my own trials. We are all guaranteed to have joys and difficulties in this life. Successful living is a process. We must continue having gratitude for the things we have accomplished. We have to accept that some dreams may not come true. And yes we still can plan for things we can still achieve.

A few people have continued to see me over the years. Some come occasionally, monthly, bi-monthly, and a very few come weekly. When I asked one young man if he wanted to quit seeing me because he was doing well, he quickly added, oh I forgot to tell you about a suicidal thought I had several weeks ago. I knew this was not true, but obviously he was not ready to be terminated. I told him he could keep coming to see me whether or not he had any bad thoughts. We scheduled another appointment.

I let people know they can always call if they get stuck, or need a mental health check-up. Just knowing they can call back if they choose to, helps to avoid all or nothing thinking. Life is composed of all shades of grey, and for some people, this is a difficult concept. Compromise is a shade of grey, and so is waiting before responding. I have learned that sometimes it is better to stop and act appropriately, rather than just react immediately. It is difficult to take something back once it is said.

My clients have taught me that I will not help everyone. People who can't or won't change have a great ability to blame me and my skills. I encourage them to move on and try someone else. I have learned that I am not a magician. I can teach people skills I have learned to deal with problems, but I can't make the pain go away. I am also aware that I am not the best fit for everyone, and that is just a fact of life. I can relate to how some of the friends and families of these people may feel. Fortunately, in many years of counseling this has been only a few clients. I do pray and ask God to remove people from my practice who are draining me, and allow those who I can help to stay. So everyone I see for counseling gets prayed for in one way or another.

I have learned from my clients that I must live what I teach. I try to model that mistakes can happen to anyone as we are all just human beings. I want to give people wings so that they can fly on their own. Finally, I believe that prayer is a powerful tool to learn. Hopefully, dear readers, my clients have also taught you something. If you have learned something from this book, I would love to hear from you. Perhaps your experiences can be part of a sequel.

www.willowcounseling.net

Acknowledgements

First, I want to thank the Lord for giving me the gifts, wisdom, and opportunity to do what I do. Next I want to thank my husband, friend, and editor, Michael Lefton. Without his years of financial and emotional support, I would not be able to do what I do. He has been my greatest cheerleader. Thank you also, to my son, who has given me many years to practice my Marlene-isms, and has forgiven my mistakes. Thanks to my mom and dad, who are now with our Lord in Heaven. They were wise, kind, and godly people who taught me how to follow in their footsteps. Lastly, thank you to all of the people who have come into my office and allowed me to be a part of their lives.